JAKE,

LITTLE JIMMY

&

BIG LOUIE

Other books by Ian Moore-Morrans

(For ordering information go to:
www.ianmooremorrans.com

or go to www.amazon.com or amazon.ca for the latter two)

METAL MACHINING MADE EASY

A DIY (do it yourself) book

(as Ian Morrans)

BEYOND THE PHANTOM BATTLE:

MYSTERY AT LOCH ASHIE

A novel of time travel and adventure

(edited by Gayle Moore-Morrans)

FROM POVERTY TO POVERTY:

A SCOTSMAN ENCOUNTERS CANADA

A memoir, 1934-1970

(edited by Gayle Moore-Morrans)

JAKE,

LITTLE JIMMY

&

BIG LOUIE

To Marilyn & Ron

A Children's Chapter Book (for Grown-ups, too)

A boy adopts and learns to love two very different birds.

with best wishes.

Ian Moore-Morrans with Gayle Moore-Morrans

Ian Moore-Morrans   *Gayle Moore-Morrans*

MOOMOR Publishing

Vernon, British Columbia, Canada

Illustrations by Great-Granddaughter Hannah German
(edited and enhanced through Microsoft Paint and
Adobe Photoshop Elements 12 by Grandma Gayle)

Age-appropriate Consultant:
Great-Grandson Leland German

ISBN 978-0-9939895-0-6 (Paperback)

ISBN 978-0-9939895-1-3 (eBook)

Book & cover design by MOOMOR Publishing

DEDICATION

To our great-grandchildren:

9-year-old Hannah German (illustrator), and

13-year-old Leland German (age-appropriate consultant);

as well as to their siblings and cousins whom we hope will
soon be old enough to enjoy this book:

Caleigh, Madison and Logan German,

Brayden and Haylee Falk,

Lexi and Alex Lee;

and to our two youngest grandchildren,

Gustav and Eva Rasen.

CONTENTS

JAKE,

LITTLE JIMMY

&

BIG LOUIE

Chapter One

Jake Wants a Pet

Every kid needs a pet. At least that's what Jake believed. Jake was 11 and would have loved a puppy for company—something he could have fun playing with when he got home from school. But he knew that his wish would never happen because of the scare his mother got when she was a little girl. She had been bitten by a dog and, since that attack, had always felt nervous and uncomfortable whenever any dog, big or small, happened to come close to her. Even tiny dogs upset her.

Finally, Jake figured he'd have to get some other kind of pet. "Maybe a rabbit," he thought. He also hoped he'd get that rabbit soon. Whenever he hinted to his mom and dad about getting a pet, his dad would say, "We'll have to wait and see." It seemed to Jake that he had been "waiting and seeing" for ages.

With spring break coming up fast, Jake knew that getting a pet before then was an absolute must. It was a "now or never" sort of thing; so he decided to ask his dad just as soon as he saw him.

Jake was taller than normal for his age, with reddish brown, curly hair. His family lived in a newer section of Vernon, a beautiful mountain-and-lake-surrounded town in the picturesque Okanagan Valley of Canada's province of British Columbia. A big plus for Jake was that their house had a big, fenced-in back yard— just ideal for his plans. He didn't have any brothers or sisters, so sometimes he felt lonely when he was not having fun with his pals. A pet, in his own words, "would be cool."

~ * ~

Jake entered the kitchen with a question: "Mom, do you know where Dad is?"

"He had to go visit a friend; then he was popping into the hardware store on his way home," Jake's mother answered as she glanced at the clock on the kitchen wall. Then she continued, "And, seeing that it's almost twelve-thirty, that's likely where he is right now."

"Will he be long?"

"I don't think so; he knows that lunch will be going on the table soon. Why? What do you want your dad for?"

Jake put on his best begging face. "Mom, would you ask Dad when he gets back if I can get a rabbit? I've asked a whole bunch of times and he keeps saying that he'll think about it. He knows I've been saving my allowance to buy a pet. Could you ask him for me? Please, Mom?"

"No way, Jake. It's between you and your father and I don't know what he'll say."

Jake didn't really listen to what his mother was saying; instead his mind filled with thoughts of a pet and the possibility of his father agreeing. He dreamily carried on, "I'd like to get one of those fluffy, white ones. You know the kind—they're called Angora, I think."

Then he brightened up a little. "I know it wouldn't be nearly as good as having a dog; but it would be okay, I guess. At least it'd be better than not having any pet. And it wouldn't bother you the way a dog might, would it?"

Then quickly, he added, "But a rabbit would be all right, wouldn't it, Mom? Nobody's scared of rabbits; are they?"

~ * ~

Jake's father arrived home just as lunch was ready. After washing his hands he sat at the table, telling Jake's mother about something funny that had gone on at the hardware store. Jake sat in silence while his mother dished up the food. His father then said grace, thanking God for the meal and immediately started talking about something else. Jake was pleased to see his father was in his usual good mood, for there was a lot of laughing going on.

He also knew his mother was well aware of what was on his mind and he hoped she would begin talking about a pet for him. She looked at Jake a few times during the meal but he wasn't sure if she was doing so for a particular reason. He decided to wait.

When they had stopped eating but were still chatting, Jake became a little impatient, thinking, 'I'm going to say something as soon as I can.'

Suddenly there was a lull in their conversation and he jumped in, again using his best begging voice. "Dad, you promised me a while ago that you'd think about letting me have a pet rabbit. Are you still thinking? You said to wait a little. So I've waited a long time and haven't been bugging you. So now do you think I could have one? Please, please? I'd really look after it and take care of it. And I'd like to get it before spring break. Please, Daddy."

"Hmm—well, Young Man, you know, I actually have given some thought to you getting a pet. But I don't know about a rabbit. They take quite a lot of looking after. There was an article in the paper just the other day about rabbits, mainly about Easter Bunnies. It told how lots of kids want a little bunny at Easter-time and then they're left to die weeks later, after the newness wears off and the interest dies down."

"I wouldn't do that, Dad; I'd really look after it, forever and ever!" Jake said excitedly.

"Forever?" his dad said with raised eyebrows. "Well, do you know the newspaper said they can live for about twelve years? That's a long time. Are you willing to look after it that long? What happens when you are, say, eighteen or nineteen, and you want to go out and spend a lot of time with your friends or go on a date with a girl friend?"

There was an uneasy silence when no one spoke. Thinking about what his dad had said made Jake look quite glum.

"So," his dad continued, looking over at Jake's mom and then back to Jake, "your mom and I have talked about this a few times since I read that article and we both know rabbits are not as easy to care for as people think. Would you consider getting a pet that isn't so much trouble, maybe something your mom and I wouldn't mind looking after when you get older? How about a little budgie?"

"*A BUDGIE*?" Jake blurted out, a little louder and with more feeling and a good deal louder voice than he had intended. Then, after a few seconds' silence, with his voice still loaded with emotion, he appealed to his father, "Oh, Da-a-ad, I don't want a silly bird! They're no fun. You can't take it for walks or throw sticks for it to fetch like you can with a dog. You can't even play with it in the back yard like you would a rabbit; it'll fly away!"

Jake certainly didn't feel very good about what his dad was saying. He was thinking, 'budgies are silly things that might be all right for girls, or maybe grown-ups, but not for boys.' He watched his dad shuffle in his chair and sip his coffee. He was waiting for some kind of indication that he didn't really have to get a budgie.

But, to his dismay, his dad continued, "A little bird like that is really no trouble to look after, you know. It's much easier to care for than a rabbit. A budgie can be a lot of fun, too. Do you know, for instance, that you can teach budgies to say things? They don't understand what is being said, mind you; but with a little patience you can have them say things like, 'My name is Joey,' 'Hello Jake' and even more things."

Jake was wide-eyed. "Are you serious, Dad? They can talk?"

"Well, not really. What you have to do is to keep repeating the same thing over and over, and some day, usually when you're not expecting it, the little budgie will come out with a few of the words you've been saying to it."

Jake was not too thrilled with the idea of looking after a "silly bird." But, knowing that his chances of getting a rabbit were not good, he thought he would play for time and ask his father some questions about budgies.

"Well, Jake, the best person to talk to would be Bill. He's that friend of mine who lives just a ways above Okanagan Lake on Bella Vista Road and owns Bill's Budgie Barn. There he raises hundreds, maybe thousands of budgies for a living. And he treats them all as if they were his own children. I'm sure he'll have all the answers for you."

"He has that many budgies? *Hundreds or thousands*?" Jake was wide-eyed.

"He certainly does. He ships them all over the country," he paused slightly, then smiled and continued. "Tell you what, Jake; we should take a drive out to see him. Then you can talk to the expert yourself and get a better idea what it's all about. How about it?"

"Okay, Dad," he replied, pretending he was interested so that he could get in his pitch for a rabbit later. "When can we see those budgies?"

Jake wasn't prepared for his father's reply. "Let's go now. It's only a short drive to Bill's place and he's always home on a Saturday." With that said, his dad got up from the chair and headed for the back door. "Coming?" he asked, as he took his hat from a coat peg and lifted the car keys off an ornamental key shelf. Opening the back door without looking at Jake or waiting for an answer, he headed out to the car.

Jake's mind was working fast, looking for a way out. 'Okay,' he thought, 'I guess I'd better go for now. Don't know what else I can do.'

* ~ * ~ *

CHAPTER TWO

Bill's Budgie Barn

A few minutes later Jake and his dad were in the car and heading west on Bella Vista Road for Bill's Budgie Barn. Despite the gorgeous views of Okanagan Lake, the distant beach and shoreline, houses and orchards scattered to the left and up the mountainside to the right, the clear blue sky and glistening water on the bay below with a few sailboats decorating the waves, Jake's head was full of budgies. Jake was surprised to realize he could not wait to get there, impatient to see "hundreds, maybe thousands" of little birds all in one place. Soon they turned into the driveway of Bill's place, parking the car behind an old red half-ton truck.

Jake got out of the car, looked all around and was sure they must be at a small farm. He saw some horses in a distant field, some cows in another and a few chickens in the yard next door.

"What's that funny smell, Dad? It's horrible."

"Well," his father replied, laughing, "it's springtime, and a farmer must have been spreading smelly manure on nearby fields. It's what I call a 'real country smell,' Son. Is it ever strong, eh? And it's anything but funny! Whew, nearly brings the tears to your eyes, doesn't it?" He was still laughing about the stink and shaking his head as they headed towards the back of the house. Jake kept his hand up to his face, pinching his nose shut.

"Dad, this must be the largest back yard around. It's lots bigger than ours, isn't it?" Jake's father was smiling at his son's excitement and the funny way he was talking while holding his nose. And there, at the end of this huge yard, was the biggest shed he had ever seen. "Wow, look at the size of that shed, Dad. It's humongous! It's nearly as big as our house!"

To one side of the yard, a very large man was walking behind a noisy red and white machine that was digging up the soil in a garden area. As the man's back was towards them, he didn't know anyone was there until Jake's dad, waving his arms, ran a little ahead of him to attract his attention. As soon as the man saw him, he shut off the noisy engine, a great big smile spreading all over his face.

"George—George Moore! Well, well, well. This sure is a pleasure. What brings you out this way?" he laughingly asked, as he removed the ear protectors keeping out the engine's loud noise. Then he shook Jake's dad's hand like he hadn't seen him for years.

"Hello Bill. It's certainly nice to see you again, too. You remember my son Jake?" As he was speaking, he nodded his head in Jake's direction. "Well, he wants a pet so I suggested we come out and have a look at your birds."

"Oh, I remember this young man all right. He's certainly grown a lot—much taller now than when I last saw him. But I didn't remember his name was Jake; I could have sworn it was John or something like that. Oh well, it's been a while, eh? How old is he now?"

"He's eleven—and yes, you're quite right, Bill. It's one of those things that happen when they're going through school. His proper name is John—John Kenneth actually. But a few years ago his school friends shortened the initials J. K. to 'Jake' and it has stuck. Anyway, I don't think there was anything we could have done about it! And he likes the nickname, so I guess it's all right. Everyone calls him Jake now; even his mom and I do."

Jake stood there smiling at this big, cheerful man whom, it seemed, he had met before, judging by the way the two grownups were talking. Jake was trying to remember him when Bill turned to face him.

"Come with me, Young Man, and I'll show you the greatest selection of birds in this part of the country. If I don't have the bird you're looking for, then no one has. Maybe you'll like the looks of one of them, for I've got lots." And with that he guided Jake towards the huge shed.

As Bill opened the door, he stepped to one side. With a sort of bow from his waist and a sweeping wave of his hand, as if Jake was a prince or something, he indicated that the boy should go inside. Jake could see that Bill was just being funny!

Jake stepped from bright sunlight into the shed's slightly darker interior, which was lit only by the light from many small windows. As the inside was a little darker than the bright sunlight, Jake couldn't see very much at first, so had to wait a few seconds to allow his eyes to adjust.

* ~ * ~ *

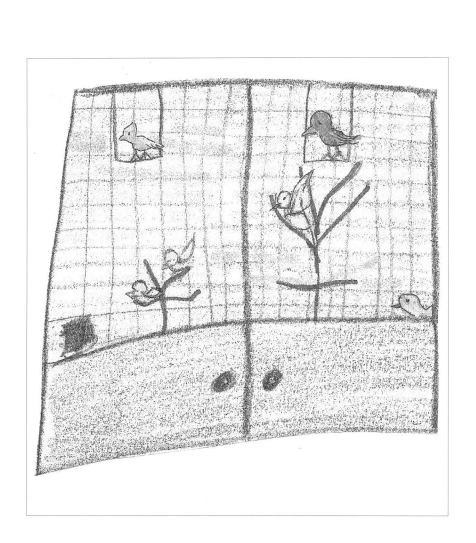

CHAPTER THREE

Jake Meets Jimmy

The first thing Jake noticed was a different smell—certainly a lot more pleasant than the one outside. Almost at the same time he heard the humming of the exhaust fans that continually changed the air inside the building to help keep the birds healthy. Next he heard lots of chirping and fluttering. And then he started noticing things. There were very large cages with a few birds in each one—rows and rows of cages—all connected end to end. Other rows were lined up on top of more rows of cages.

There were long, wide passages on either side of each row to allow lots of room to walk between them. Then he saw the birds! There actually were hundreds of the most beautiful birds he had ever seen—green, yellow and blue budgies everywhere he looked. 'WOW,' he thought, 'this is awesome!'

Bill stayed by the door talking with Jake's dad while the boy slowly made his way along one of the passages, looking at and, he had to admit, admiring the beautiful birds. Some were sitting on their perches and others were flying from one level to another.

All of a sudden, Jake stopped, stared and thought, 'That's weird!' One little bird that was walking on the floor of its cage grabbed his attention. For some reason it seemed different and he could not quite see why. Jake stood staring at the budgie for what seemed ages. Then suddenly, it dawned on him; THE LITTLE BIRD HAD NO WINGS! Where there should have been wings, there was—nothing! 'Man, that's creepy.' he thought. 'All birds should be able to fly, shouldn't they?'

Jake didn't know how to react; it seemed like he was glued to the spot. He felt so sorry for it. About all he could do was look at the poor little bird. He was totally unaware that he had slowly knelt down by the cage and was making soft, clicking noises, trying to get it to come closer.

As he knelt on the cold concrete, the next thing Jake felt was a man's hand lightly resting on his shoulder. Bill had crouched down beside him; and Jake, being so engrossed with the little budgie, hadn't even noticed.

"That's Jimmy," the big man said. Then his voice sounded a bit sad. "There are so many birds in here that it was weeks after he hatched before I noticed he was different. I didn't have the heart to end his little life; I figured that no one would want to buy a budgie that has no wings."

"I'll buy him," Jake said suddenly.

"If I thought you were serious, I'd give him to you if you'd promise to look after him. He seems to be a smart little guy. But why on earth would you want a bird that can't fly, Jake?"

"Why would I want a bird that can't fly?" Jake smiled at Bill and with a twinkle in his eye, said, "Well, we're really a lot alike. You see, I can't fly either!"

Bill laughed. "Aha! You're a bit of a comic, too, I see! Okay, Funny Guy; he's yours. And you know what, Young Man? Seeing as you've shown some compassion today, I think you deserve a reward. I'm going to give you a nice birdcage to keep him in."

"Thanks, that's great! Does that mean that I can take him home today?" Bill nodded.

Then Jake hesitated for a moment and a strange look slowly appeared on his face. "Can I ask a question?"

"Sure, Jake, go ahead."

"How come Jimmy has no wings and all the other birds do?"

The big man looked around, and then sat down on a nearby wooden box to be more at eye level with the boy. He looked a little bit uneasy and thought for a few moments. Then, gesturing to the boy to sit on another nearby box, he settled himself to give the boy a detailed explanation. After a moment's pause he shrugged his shoulders, finally deciding that a simple answer would be the best for the time being.

"Jake," he almost stammered, finding it difficult to know what to say, "it could be damage from the environment, or—if you've heard of genes—maybe one of his genes developed wrong. We still have lots to learn about this subject and only God has the answers. But the main thing for people like you and me, I'd say, is in how we act towards something, or someone, with a problem like Jimmy's. It's important that we don't consciously make them feel different."

He sighed again as he got to his feet. "Oh, you'll learn more later; it's enough to say that our little friend Jimmy is not going to make it on his own in the bird world. He certainly needs someone like you who would really care for him." Bill hesitated just a little, then very earnestly while looking straight at Jake said, "If you take him home, you should be sure that it's something you really want to do. It's very important that you don't do it just because you feel sorry for him. Okay?"

Jake looked again at the tiny green and yellow bird and thought, 'He does seem to be a cool little guy. It's good he's coming home with me; I'll look after him.'

"It's okay, Bill," he said out loud. "I promise I'll take very good care of him."

~ * ~

Before they left for home, Bill also gave Jake a supply of bird seed, a tiny bell that hangs from the top of the cage for the bird to 'ping' with his beak, a little ladder, plus water and seed dishes to clip onto the inside of the cage.

Jake decided that he wouldn't change Jimmy's name as it seemed to suit him just fine. After they visited with Bill for a few more minutes, Jake and his dad said their thanks and goodbyes and headed for home. Jimmy was comfortably settled in his new cage which had been buckled into the back seat.

* ~ * ~ *

CHAPTER FOUR

A Super-Duper,

Jimmy-Go-Up-And-Down Ramp

As they headed home, Jake and his dad chatted about their visit to Bill's Budgie Barn and all they had seen there. When the car was in the garage, his dad took the birdcage from the back seat and began heading for the house, carefully carrying it by its handle.

"Where do you want your new friend?" Dad asked Jake. "Downstairs in the living room with us or up in your bedroom?"

"In my bedroom, I think, Dad. That way I can talk to him like you said and I won't disturb anyone."

"Okay, that's good thinking. First of all, though, let's take him to show to your mom. Then we'll see what we can do upstairs."

After Jake's mom got over the surprise of seeing a budgie with no wings, she "oohed and aahed" over the little bird. Then Jimmy, Jake and his dad headed upstairs. Looking around the bedroom for the perfect place, his father finally pointed toward the window.

Jake's chest of drawers was in front of the window, and its top was level with the windowsill, an ideal spot. Jake's dad remarked, "I think you should take those things off the top of your chest of drawers and we'll put Jimmy and his cage up there. He'll be able to see out to the back yard, especially early in the morning before you get up for school."

After some of Jake's junk had been cleared away and the cage was put into place, his dad gave Jake a list of things to gather from the basement workshop including cardboard, a utility knife, a pair of scissors, a stapler, duct tape, a tube of glue and some sheets of sandpaper.

'Wow, what a list!' Jake thought. 'I wonder why Dad wants all this stuff just for a little bird. ' When he got back upstairs, with most of the stuff crammed into an old grocery bag, Jake found that some of his furniture had been moved around. Even his bed had been moved to another wall and his dad had put a chair close to Jimmy's cage.

Jake sat at the bottom of the bed and followed his dad's instructions to cut the cardboard into strips, folding it at various places. Then, with his dad using the glue and stapler, Jake folded some more cardboard, while his dad glued and stapled again and again until they had a few lengths of what looked to Jake like a miniature slide.

As Jake imagined Jimmy going down the slide, he started giggling to himself. 'Dad says I can teach him to speak, so maybe he could learn to say "wheeeeee," too. It would be really neat to see Jimmy going down the slide and going "Wheeee"!' But when his dad glued sandpaper strips onto the insides of the bottom of the structure, Jake was no longer sure about the slide.

"What is this thing, Dad?" he asked, trying not to laugh. "I thought it was a slide; but now I'm not so sure!"

"This, son, is a 'super-duper, Jimmy-go-up-and-down ramp'! We can tape each section to various places to allow your new friend to hop from your dresser down to the chair, and then from the chair to the floor. This one we're making now goes from the floor up to the bottom of your bed. What do you think of that? The sides are to give it strength, so it won't buckle, and the sandpaper will give his little feet a grip so that he won't slip."

I see." But Jake was still a bit puzzled. "You said it's to let him get down to the floor?"

"That's right. The ramps will let Jimmy investigate his new home. This means you must be sure that you always know where he is or you may step on him. I'm sure you wouldn't want to do that! You can leave his cage door open and, as he can't fly, at least he'll have some freedom."

"Hey, that's terrific, Dad," Jake eagerly replied. "That means he's not like a prisoner anymore. Right?"

"Right!"

~ * ~

Jake's dad gathered up his tools saying, "I'll leave you and Jimmy to get to know each other, so Mom and I probably won't see you 'til suppertime. There's one thing you need to remember, though; and it's really important. Make sure Jimmy is safely in his cage and the cage door is closed every night before you go to bed. That way he'll be somewhere secure and safe throughout the night, because the first time he gets stepped on will most likely be his last time, too. Understand?"

"Sure, Dad, I promise ..." Jake hesitated. "Dad, do you think maybe God made Jimmy especially for me?"

Why not?" His father answered. "Anything's possible. You can ask yourself why you just 'happened' to be there today of all days to take him home before someone else did."

"Hey, that's neat. And Dad, thanks for doing all this."

"Oh, you're welcome, Son." And, with that, Jake's dad went out, giving Jake a little wink and a smile as he closed the bedroom door behind him.

CHAPTER FIVE

Jake and Jimmy Become Friends

Jake held his face close to the bars of the cage as he examined his new pet. "Well, Jimmy, you certainly don't look like a rabbit! But, seeing as I stuck my neck out by saying that I would take you, I guess I'll just have to make the best of it. But you might as well know right now, I'd still rather have had a rabbit!"

As Jimmy cocked his head from side to side, Jake watched the budgie for a few moments more, and then opened the cage door. Next, sitting on his bed, he slid around until his back was against the headboard, with his hands folded on his chest. Propped up this way he was able to watch Jimmy, wondering if he would actually use the ramp.

The bird stayed in the cage and looked around the room. Jake kept watching and waiting. It took a little while, maybe two minutes, then Jimmy hopped out of his cage and onto the top of the chest of drawers. Hesitating for a moment, he again looked around at his new surroundings, then finally at Jake. Next he hopped, very slowly—and sort of sideways—down the first ramp.

Jimmy "chirp, chirp, chirped" off and on as he gradually made his way downward. It wasn't long 'til he was on the chair, and then he continued down to the floor. Hopping over to the ramp that led up to the footboard of Jake's bed, he started to climb. With more "chirp, chirp, chirps," he was soon on the bed! Jimmy watched the boy most of the time as he was hopping, all the while cocking his head from side to side the way budgies do. He let out a few more "chirp, chirp, chirps" as he hopped over the covers of the bed toward Jake. Jake didn't move; he didn't want to scare the little bird. Then Jimmy used his beak and claws on Jake's clothes to pull himself up onto Jake's lap. He looked once more at Jake, then hopped over and onto Jake's folded hands.

Jimmy perched there, motionless, looking up at his new owner. Jake didn't move. Still looking up at Jake, Jimmy "chirp-chirped" once more. Well, that just made Jake's day! He was sure that Jimmy was somehow saying, "Thank you."

Something really good happened to Jake just then. A "strange, warm, loving feeling" was how he would later describe it.

From that moment on, Jimmy became very important to Jake, almost like they were best friends.

'Just imagine me telling the guys at school that my best friend is a budgie! NO WAY!' Jake thought. But secretly he knew it was true.

~ * ~

Spring break was soon over. As the weeks went by, Jake hurried straight home from school each day, immediately heading for his bedroom.

Remembering what his dad had said about keeping Jimmy safe, Jake would open the door very slowly, in case Jimmy was close to it.

All the while that Jake was opening the door and as he came into the room, he would say, "Hi Jake, hi Jake, hi Jake," so that, hopefully, Jimmy would hear and repeat it.

Jake had been saying "Hi Jake!" and "Jimmy's a good boy!" over and over to Jimmy in the past weeks, hoping that he would finally repeat something.

Then, one day as he slowly opened his bedroom door while saying, "Hi, Jake," a little high voice from somewhere over there said, "Hi Jake, hi Jake."

Jake was thrilled. 'My little bird can speak. Wow!'

Jake looked around and discovered his pet on the floor beside the bed. Going over to the bed, he sat on the edge and picked up Jimmy very carefully.

Jimmy immediately hopped onto his lap and started to climb up Jake's sweater. Using his beak and claws, he gradually pulled himself up until he was perched on Jake's left shoulder, saying, "Hi Jake, hi Jake."

Well, Jake couldn't have been happier. This little bird of his was certainly the best little budgie in the whole world!

"Hey! Who needs a dog or a rabbit? Not me!" Jake said laughingly. He surely had the best pet in the world!

* ~ * ~ *

CHAPTER SIX

A Park Outing Goes Wrong

One day Jake's parents came home from shopping with a small travel cage for Jimmy. They had seen it at the Salvation Army store, their favourite place to shop for special things. Perhaps it would be useful if Jake ever wanted to take Jimmy to the vet or out to the back yard. Jake agreed that it was great and would come in handy.

After a few trips to the back yard, Jimmy learned to hop right into the travel cage when Jake put it beside him. It seemed to Jake that Jimmy knew when he was going to go outside to the grass, because he rushed to get into the cage as soon as Jake opened the door for him. That was when Jake remembered Bill saying that Jimmy was a "smart little guy."

Then Jake got braver, or maybe more careless, judging by what happened next. When his best pals, Brien, Eugene and Eugene's one-year-younger sister Tiffany came over, the four of them would head to a nearby park with Jimmy in his travel cage. They would sit in a little circle on the grass with Jimmy's small cage in the middle. Jake would open the cage door, allowing Jimmy to come out and hop about the area among them. Their usual spot was close enough to the pond to watch the ducks, but far enough away from the water so that Jimmy was in no danger. They did this quite often when the weather was nice and they all agreed that Jimmy probably enjoyed it as much as they did!

~ * ~

One day, during the early part of September, the four "amigos," with Jimmy wandering around them, were sitting enjoying a sunny Saturday afternoon on the soft grass at their usual spot in the park. Suddenly they heard a woman's voice shouting, "Stop him; stop that boy. He's got my purse."

As their heads turned in the direction of the voice, they saw a boy, not much older than they were, running along the path at the other side of the pond and almost in their direction, clutching a lady's handbag.

"C'mon, you three. Let's get that guy!" Brien shouted as the thief ran past them. With that, the four of them jumped to their feet.

There wasn't enough time to put Jimmy into his cage, so Jake scooped him up and tucked him into his jacket pocket. They then started racing as fast as they could after the thief.

Twisting around bushes, trees and flowerbeds while running over a large section of the park, Jake gradually outdistanced his friends because of his longer legs. He was quite a bit in front when suddenly the thief, who knew that he was soon going to get caught, threw away the purse. Jake didn't let up. He was just a very short distance behind the thief when the boy suddenly turned on him, putting his fists up, ready for a fight. Two seconds before they were about to clash, Jake quickly bent over and with his head lowered, rammed the thief in the middle of his chest.

Having the wind knocked out of him, the thief was taken by surprise. He and Jake fell to the ground, wrestling as they rolled around. The next thing Jake knew was that Tiffany had joined the scuffle, grabbing hold of the thief's hair. Battling the pair, the thief didn't have much strength to fight after Jake had plowed into him. This made it easy for Jake and Tiffany to hold him down until Jake's other two friends and two nearby adults arrived on the scene.

In the meantime, the lady had retrieved her purse from where the thief had thrown it. Soon she was headed to the police station along with the two adults who were holding on to the thief and nudging him along.

Since Jake and Tiffany had finished off their tackling of the thief by rolling into one of the flowerbeds, their clothes were really dirty. Getting to his feet and, beginning to wipe himself off, Jake suddenly thought, 'Jimmy!' In all the excitement, Jake had forgotten all about his little pet. His hand flashed to his jacket pocket. It was empty!

CHAPTER SEVEN

Little Jimmy is Lost!

Jake panicked, his heart missing a beat and tears filling his eyes. He'd lost his best friend! Had Jimmy been crushed when Jake was rolling on the ground? Was he close by or nearer to where they'd started running? Where could Jimmy be? Was he still alive? Had some passerby stepped on him? All of these questions raced through Jake's mind, making him fear the worst.

They had covered a lot of ground, running here and there and around bushes as they chased the thief. Jimmy could have fallen out anywhere in between. Not only was Jimmy tiny; he was also mostly yellow and green—a perfect camouflage, making it very difficult to see him in the grass!

"Hey guys, I've lost my Jimmy," Jake called out. He found it hard to talk, to tell them to be careful where they stepped in case they would hurt him. They had covered a lot of ground and Jake knew it would be very difficult to retrace their actual route.

Eugene took over. "Okay guys, we'll spread out and slowly go back to where we started. Don't worry, Jake; we'll find him for you."

The four started to retrace their steps, going back gradually to where they had been sitting. They zigzagged back and forth, all the time quietly calling, "Jimmy, where are you? Jimmy? ... Jimmy?"

During the search, Tiffany approached a group of boys and girls about their own age who were playing in the area, explained what Jimmy looked like and asked them to help look for the little bird. With the extra help, Jake felt a bit better. Five extra pairs of eyes could make a difference and the more people that were looking for Jimmy, the more hopeful Jake became that they would find him.

"Jimmy, where are you?" Jake called out continuously. He had a strange lump in his throat and felt so terrible to have lost his little friend that he could scarcely get out the words.

It was more than an hour later and they were almost back to where they had started the chase; but still there was no sign of

Jimmy. When they reached the spot, Jake got another shock; Jimmy's cage was gone!

"Hey guys, look—Jimmy's cage has been stolen. This is where we were, isn't it?" he said, turning around and around, looking, and trying to confirm their spot. "It *is* where we were, isn't it?"

"This is where we were, for sure." Brien said. "But we should slowly go back again to where we started the search, right where we caught the thief. We should search again and again 'til we find him. Maybe we'll get the cage later."

"Yes, you're right, Brien; but why would anyone steal Jimmy's little cage?" Everyone shrugged their shoulders.

They found some more kids nearby who also joined the search. There were now 14 kids searching everywhere for Jimmy, but not a trace of him could be found. They looked again and again all over the area where they had chased the thief, but eventually had to give up because it was beginning to get dark.

~ * ~

Once Jake was home and reported to his parents what had happened, Dad had an explanation. "Somebody has stolen Jimmy," he stated. "You searched the whole area for two hours and didn't find any trace of him. Right? You know that Jimmy was trained to go into his cage. Right? This tells me that Jimmy must have fallen out as soon as you put him in your pocket, and when he couldn't see you, he headed for 'home.' He went into his cage, where he felt safe. Someone must have come along, picked up the cage with Jimmy in it and just kept on going. Either that or a passer-by, seeing no one around, found him and thought he'd been left there intentionally."

"Oh, Dad, that's awful! How can we get him back? Do you think we can?"

"First thing we do is go to the police station and let them know what's happened. We'll find out when we go there if he's been turned in. Next thing we do is put an ad in the paper, hoping someone reads it that knows of a person who has just acquired a wingless budgie, or even just any budgie. We may get some sort of response—at least it's worth a try. I'll do it right away."

After they visited the police station and wrote out a report, Jake felt better, hoping it would do some good.

~ * ~

A week later, Jake's dad walked out the back door with a great big smile on his face as he approached Jake, Brien and Tiffany, who were playing in the back yard.

"I've got big news, guys! There's been a call from a man who knows someone who has just become the owner of a budgie in a little cage. It seems like the ad in the paper has paid off."

This, of course, caused the three kids to jump up in the air with glee, bouncing around and hugging each other.

Mr. Moore then called the police to report the phone number of the person who had called him. The police sergeant at the desk informed Jake's dad that they would investigate and get back to him as soon as they visited the person who had a new budgie and found out whether or not it was Jimmy.

CHAPTER EIGHT

"Jimmy's a Good Boy"

The following day, two police constables were at Jake's house along with Jimmy who was safely in his cage. Jake was in orbit over the news that Jimmy had been found, for he had hardly slept that whole week while Jimmy was missing. Lying awake in his bed at night, he had prayed that Jimmy would be kept safe, wherever he was, and that Jimmy would come home soon. He promised to love Jimmy and always try to take very good care of him. This promise had kept him certain that Jimmy would be found, so when Jake's father told him the good news, he sort of expected it. 'Well' he thought, 'it got Jimmy back to me.'

The police told Jake that the budgie and his cage had been sold to an older lady. The lady couldn't identify the seller and could only tell them that someone at her door had offered it cheap.

The good news was that Jimmy was okay and now Jake had him at home. As soon as Jimmy saw Jake, he immediately chirped out, "Hi, Jake."

Jake answered with, "Hi, Jimmy" and then, "Jimmy's a good boy."

And was Jake ever surprised when Jimmy repeated, "Jimmy's a good boy. Jimmy's a good boy," over and over again.

Jake smiled at Jimmy's new words and admitted to himself that if Jimmy had been bigger, he would have given him a great big hug. (He didn't tell anyone that he was thinking, 'Jake loves Jimmy; Jake loves Jimmy.' He just couldn't tell that to anyone, especially his pals!)

From that day onward, it seemed as if Jimmy were glued to Jake's left shoulder pretty much all of the time. Other things didn't seem to matter much to the little bird. He perched there from the time Jake lifted him up, only taking a break to get a drink or some seed, but never moving very far from his favourite spot.

Jake thought that possibly Jimmy had got hurt a little when he fell to the ground and had to wait until he healed. He seemed all right, but budgies are so small, that sometimes it was hard to tell just how Jimmy felt. Jimmy might also have realized that something scary had happened to him, and it would probably take him a while to get back to normal.

The budgie had been home more than a month before he recovered from whatever was bothering him. One day shortly after Jake put Jimmy up onto his left shoulder, Jimmy finally went back to doing his "old" routine, running over to the other shoulder, about-facing and going down Jake's right sleeve backwards, using his claws and beak, just about as fast as he could.

This was likely caused by Jake going to the cupboard to get out a soda cracker. Jimmy just loved soda crackers and Jake had made a habit of feeding him one now and then, although it made an awful mess with crumbs all over the place.

Jimmy had been silent since he had said those few words when he first saw Jake again after he'd been lost. Jake knew that Jimmy could smell a soda cracker from a long way off but he didn't think when Jimmy got that cracker that it would have the effect it did. Now, as soon as he finished his cracker, Jimmy started repeating, "Jimmy's a good boy; Jimmy's a good boy."

Jake thought it was great fun listening to Jimmy chatter. He was glad that he had been the one to take Jimmy home from Bill's Budgie Barn, not someone else. He was so thankful that

Jimmy was home again, safe and sound and that he seemed to have recovered from the shock of being lost, then stolen and sold, and finally returned by the police constables.

Ah, life with Jimmy was back to normal and Jake was certain that they were going to continue to have a really good time together.

~~*

CHAPTER NINE

"Thing" Arrives

Some months later, the week after Jake's twelfth birthday, another problem appeared. And Jake was sure a certain kid was the cause of everything getting all messed up again. As far as Jake was concerned, he didn't want to go through any more troubles. But that little kid appeared at his door and sure screwed things up for Jake in a BIG way!

Now Jake's Grandpa was an old Scotsman who loved the poetry of the even-older Scotsman, named Robert Burns. Even Dad had started quoting some old sayings of Burns, so it wasn't surprising that a phrase from Burns' poem, "To a Mouse" came into Jake's mind. He had often heard both Grandpa and Dad say something like, "The best laid schemes o' mice an' men gang aft a-gley"– meaning that you can make really good plans but they can often go wrong. However it was stated, Jake thought, the saying must apply to 12-year-old boys too, for things certainly did go wrong for Jake—well, for a little while anyway.

~ * ~

Here is how things began to go wrong. Jake had just returned home after visiting his friends when he heard an awful noise coming from the back door.

"Jake, please see who is making that racket!" his mother called just as Jake started to head in that direction.

Somebody was kicking at the back door really hard, and just wouldn't let up. When Jake threw open the door, he was surprised to see a young boy, maybe seven or eight years old, standing there clutching something to his chest. His hands were cupped one on top of the other, making a hollow sort of container with something hidden inside. As both his hands were busy, the kid couldn't knock or use the doorbell so he had to kick, and Jake was just about to bawl him out for it.

But before Jake could say anything, the boy shoved something into Jake's hands. "Here," he said, "take this. I don't know what to do with it and you know all about birds." Then he was gone.

It all happened so fast that somehow, without thinking, Jake had unconsciously held out his hands when the kid reached out towards him. Jake looked at what he had just received and was flabbergasted, thinking, 'this has got to be the ugliest thing I've ever seen in my whole life.'

It was a baby bird of some sort, quite naked with just a bit of fuzz here and there. Its eyes were closed and it felt so cold that Jake was sure it was dead. He didn't know what to do next. As he stood there looking at the poor thing, it moved a little.

'Hey, this thing's alive,' he realized. Quickly closing the door and hurrying as fast as his legs could take him, Jake looked for his parents, hoping that they would know what to do.

"Dad, Mom, I need your help, quick. Look at what some little kid just gave me; and the thing is still alive. Can you tell me what to do? I've got to feed 'Thing' or he'll die." Jake sounded a little panicky, but he couldn't help it, as nothing like this had ever happened to him before.

"Well, it sounds like Thing already has a name, eh?" Dad replied. "I don't know too much about feeding baby birds."

Jake's mom shook her head and agreed. "I don't know either Jake; but it does look as though Thing is almost dead."

Then Dad came up with a course of action. "Let's phone Bill and see what he says. There's a chance he'll also know something about wild birds. Let's hope he's home. You can tell him that we've no idea what kind of bird it is, except that it's too large a chick to be a sparrow. It must have fallen out of its nest."

~ * ~

By the fourth ring, Bill's answering machine cut in. 'Oh, no, please,' Jake thought, 'I don't need this. I need help now!' Then part way through the message, Bill lifted the phone, and his "real" voice answered.

"Bill's Budgie Barn. Bill speaking. May I help you?"

"Hello Bill, this is Jake Moore. You know, the boy that got little Jimmy from you last year. Some kid just handed me an almost-dead baby bird, that I'm calling Thing. It hasn't been long since Thing was hatched and it's pretty cold. Dad says that maybe you can tell me how to feed Thing. We don't know what kind of wild bird it is but it's bigger than a sparrow. It doesn't have feathers yet, just a bit of fuzz."

* ~ * ~ *

CHAPTER TEN

Poor Little "Thing"

It was good that the owner of "Bill's Budgie Barn" knew all about caring for baby birds, not just budgies—but even wild birds. First, Bill told Jake to wrap Thing in something warm like an oven mitt. He then suggested placing Thing and the mitt on the kitchen stovetop, switching the oven on low and leaving the oven door slightly open to allow some heat to float up and warm the air around the bird. Then, while the chick was getting warmed up, Jake was to cook an egg in boiling water until it was just soft boiled, about three minutes.

With the help of an eyedropper, Jake was pleased that the bird managed to take in a little water. As the boy waited for the egg to boil, he spoke to the half-dead chick, now cradled in an old woolen glove. Its eyes were still closed.

"Okay, Thing, you know I really should ignore you. Then you'd die and I wouldn't have to spend time looking after you. But,

..., well ..., if I do that, then I'd be responsible for killing you, and I know I'd feel really lousy if that happened. But, you see, I don't want another bird. I have my little Jimmy and that's enough for me. Oh heck, I guess I've got no choice except to try to keep you alive."

Jake wasn't sure if the chick was listening. The egg was cooked, cooled and mashed up, ready to be eaten. So now all Jake had to do was figure out how to get some of the mashed egg inside the bird.

When Jake set the egg down next to Thing, the baby bird didn't even move. It became obvious to Jake that the only way Thing was going to get some food was to somehow force-feed it. "Poor little Thing, poor little Thing. C'mon, eat something." Jake tried to coax it. To begin with, Thing's eyes were still closed so Jake had to help it as much as possible.

With tweezers and a toothpick, he put some tiny bits into the bird's mouth. Thing did take some in, but not much. All Jake could do after that was hope it was getting enough to keep it alive! He switched the oven off and lifted the glove, cradling the chick inside it. After he did so, he tucked it inside his shirt, using his own body heat to keep it nice and warm. Then he found a small box, placed the glove with the chick inside the box and took everything upstairs to his bedroom, so Jimmy could see the newcomer.

~ * ~

Every morning for the first week, as soon as he woke up, Jake would jump out of bed and look to see how the poor little chick was doing; expecting to see it had died during the night. But, strangely, he was always relieved to see that Thing was okay. Then he would leave Jimmy in charge and run down to the 'fridge to get some of the left-over mashed-up egg and warm a little of it just a bit in the microwave, rush back upstairs again and feed Thing. As each day passed, Thing seemed a little more alive. By the end of the second week he was actually making an attempt at standing on his own two feet.

Jimmy would never come too close to Thing, but just watched his progress from the safety of Jake's shoulder. Baby Thing was already getting bigger than fully-grown Jimmy!

Thing wasn't very good at eating at the beginning; but it certainly wasn't long before he learned exactly what to do. As the days went by, he ate more and more on his own, grew a lot more feathers and began to look more and more like a bird. But—and a big "but" it was—Thing started to look more and more like a crow!

Jake was downhearted. 'Gee,' he thought, 'did it have to be an ugly old crow? Couldn't it have been something else; like maybe a lark or a robin? Crows are ugly and noisy.

Though Jake had never really wanted a bird of any sort when he first got Jimmy, it didn't take long for him to become very fond of his little budgie. Now he wouldn't part with him. So much so, in fact, Jimmy was the only pet Jake really wanted. Now it seemed like the boy had inherited this other bird, which, at first, had looked more like a mini-prehistoric monster than a chick! But Jake had committed himself to looking after it, and look after it he must do, even if it was only to satisfy his own conscience.

"I sure don't want this horrible-looking Thing," he said out loud to Jimmy. "That little kid—Pffft!—I wonder how he happened to find a crow chick! How come he knew that I had a little bird of my own? Oh, I wish that that kid, whoever he is, had left well enough alone."

Yes, Jake thought he would have been a much happier boy if that kid had never set eyes on the baby bird! And now, although he was concerned about keeping the bird alive, he wanted it so little that he didn't even give it a proper name, except to think of it as "Thing!" He just wanted to keep it alive until it was able to fly away, taking Jake's problem with it.

What happened after that would not concern him one bit, he thought.

But, boy was Jake wrong!

* ~ * ~ *

CHAPTER ELEVEN

"Thing" Becomes "Louie"

Meanwhile, Jimmy had kept Jake well entertained with his constant "talking" which had really become quite good. Jake had become accustomed to wandering all around the house with Jimmy almost continuously perched on his favourite place, Jake's left shoulder. That was where Jimmy was content to remain, for he could see quite a lot from up there.

It also meant that Jimmy was with Jake most of the time while he was looking after Thing. Thus, Jimmy had some, if small, connection with the ugly bird—as there wasn't usually much distance between them when the frequent feeding times came.

It seemed like Thing was always looking for food, beak open and waving in the air as if it constantly needed a refill. Thing could also make quite a bit of noise by now, especially when it was hungry; for it let out squawks that sounded like "ouie, ouie, ouie."

Jake would get food for Thing, go to the cage and then say "ouie, ouie, ouie," to signal that the food was there. Then, one day he suddenly realized that the call from the newcomer sounded more like, "Louie, Louie, Louie."

Suddenly the ugly bird had a name, a real name; and it wasn't even one of Jake's choosing! The bird was saying it loud and clear, too, which wasn't very good in Jake's opinion.

Why? Well, Jake knew that, when a person gave a name to an animal, that meant the person was getting more attached to it. He had thought of naming it, maybe calling it "Blackie" because of the shiny black feathers that were sprouting all over it. But he decided against it. He didn't really want it to have a name and that was that; or so he thought!

But situations change when that something tells you its own name. Then it's certainly a different story. Here was this bird, just a little more than a baby, and it could repeat its name to Jake.

'Okay,' Jake thought to himself, 'tomorrow I'll have to get myself to the library and find out what I can about crows, since Louie seems to be a crow.'

The next day was Saturday. Jake was at the Vernon Library first thing in the morning, waiting for the doors to open. Once inside, one of the staff helped him look for books about birds. There were quite a few to choose from. He picked two he thought might be helpful, taking both of them home to study.

In a book that told about identifying birds, Jake learned that he didn't have a crow; he had a RAVEN! Also, as if his bird problem wasn't big enough, the other book described a raven as being a lot bigger than a crow. Its wingspan (measuring from the tip of one wing to the tip of the other wing) was called "massive," much bigger than Jimmy's would have been if he'd had any wings. To Jake's surprise, the book also informed him that ravens were very intelligent birds!

So, what Jake actually had was a large, *smart* bird; though he thought he didn't really care whether it was smart or not. However, Jake would soon learn that Louie himself would show Jake just how smart he really was!

Upon learning that a raven's wingspan could reach about two feet when fully grown, Jake was afraid he wouldn't know what he would do with such a large bird. All he wanted was for Louie to grow big enough to fly away. He was going to be a GIANT compared with little Jimmy.

* ~ * ~ *

CHAPTER TWELVE

Louie Gives Jake a BIG Problem

When Jake first got the almost-naked, half-dead little chick handed to him at his door, it wasn't much smaller than Jimmy was fully grown. Pretty soon Louie was bigger than Jimmy and still growing. After the egg diet was finished, Jake found that a young raven would eat just about anything. Any table scraps in the house soon disappeared.

One day when Jake and his father were talking about Louie's appetite, his dad jokingly said that ravens only turned their noses up at car license plates, hubcaps and rusty nails. That was sort of true, too; Jake never had any trouble finding something for Louie to eat!

The boy watched as the raven matured more each day. Jake could almost see Louie getting bigger as the days wore on. He guessed that it might only be two to three weeks before Louie would be able to fly; and off he would go.

'Goody-goody,' Jake thought, 'I can't wait.' But, in the meantime, he had to get a bigger cage than the little travel cage to keep the big bird in.

Things didn't go quite as planned for Jake; in fact, not anywhere close to where he could even have imagined they might go. It would soon be the second time in a short while that the saying about "mice and men's plans" was going to ring true for him.

~ * ~

Well . . . maybe some of the blame should go to the budgie, Jimmy. You see, all the time, whenever Jake was feeding Louie, Jimmy would be on his shoulder, chattering away like crazy. He had become quite a good talker by this time. Very often he sounded like a recording, as he came out with, "Jimmy's a good boy, Jimmy's a good boy" or "Jimmy loves Jake" or one of the other new sayings he was learning.

Louie was getting bigger and stronger and constantly flapping his wings. That meant he was exercising and strengthening his muscles. Soon Louie would have strong enough muscles so that he could take flight and fly away.

'Goodie. Not long now,' Jake thought. He was getting desperate for that day to arrive.

So, here was this giant of a bird compared to little Jimmy, and Jake was getting ready to feed him. As he approached with the food, Jake gave the signal, "Louie, Louie, Louie."

"Jimmy's a good boy, Jimmy's a good boy." The sound had come from down where Louie was.

Jake was taken aback. 'What's this?' he thought. It sounded like Louie was speaking. It couldn't be Jimmy. He was on Jake's shoulder. Another thing too, the sound wasn't as high-pitched as Jimmy's voice! Surely it couldn't be? A raven couldn't "talk," could it?

"Jimmy's a good boy, Jimmy's a good boy." There it was again. Louie was saying it, and Jake couldn't believe it. He'd never ever heard of a raven being able to do anything like that. He had learned by now that almost all the different birds of the parrot family could be trained to say lots of funny things. Some species were better at it than others; but he certainly didn't know that ravens could learn to talk, too!

'What should I do now?' he thought. He had been waiting for Louie to get big and strong so that he would be able to fly off on his own. Then the bird would be in its own natural environment and things could get back to normal—back to where they were before that little kid appeared and thrust that half-dead chick into Jake's hands.

Jake looked at Louie, stared him straight in the eyes and, speaking out loud to him, put on a tough guy accent. "Okay, Louie; it looks like I've got to find out a lot more about ravens, eh? Maybe a phone call to Bill's Budgie Barn might help."

Bill couldn't help Jake very much except to confirm that he had occasionally heard of people teaching ravens to say some words. He had never personally heard a raven "talking," except for one time he himself had heard one in the wilderness imitating a cuckoo!

~ * ~

You can't really talk to a bird, whether it's a little budgie or a very large parrot, and ask it questions, or have a conversation with it. It works something like a tape recorder, not nearly as efficient, but a lot more fun. You have to repeat the same thing over and over and over again and someday (maybe) the bird might repeat what you say, although it wouldn't know what the words meant.

Anyway, it was obvious to Jake that he had to do some serious talking with himself! By learning to "speak" a few words, Louie had caused Jake to look at him differently. Jake now looked at this big bird with a bit of admiration. Maybe "respect" would be a better word; for before this, he certainly had little respect for Louie. What Jake had seen prior to this was nothing more than a big, scraggy-looking eating machine that he hoped would soon go away!

~ * ~

Now it seemed that Jake had another problem he didn't need. Louie was getting very big. The big bird practiced flapping his wings whenever he was out of his cage. Jake had been looking forward so much to having Louie fly away, but now he wasn't so sure he wanted to see Louie go.

'Well, Jake,' he said to himself, 'another week or so and he'll be gone, so you'd better make up your mind what you are going to do about him.'

Jake wasn't very clever in thinking that; he realized almost right away that he really had nothing to say about whether Louie left or stayed. The decision would have to be strictly Louie's; and Jake didn't doubt what that would be. Louie would "find his wings," as they say, take flight and off he would go. It really made no difference whether he could "talk" a bit or not!

In the meantime, little Jimmy had become quite attached to the big bird and loved to play with him. Sometimes, when they were close together, Jake would get a little scared, especially when the two of them were on the basement floor playing with each other. Louie was so big compared to Jimmy that Jake often thought something might happen to injure Jimmy because of their difference in size, but it never did.

Jimmy and Louie had become really good buddies as they raced along the floor together. Jake had a lot of fun just watching them. Louie would hop a little, stop, look around to see where Jimmy was and, as soon as Jimmy caught up to him, off he would go again, teasing his little friend!

There was something unusual Louie would do that Jake found quite fascinating. He would sort-of squat, with his body low on the floor and his eyes closed, so that Jimmy would be about level with Louie's head. Then Jimmy would do a funny clicking with his beak against Louie's huge beak.

Jake could distinctly hear the "click, click, click" of the two beaks hitting together as Jimmy rapidly tapped his small beak against Louie's big, black beak. Louie never moved all the time this clicking was going on; you'd think he was frozen to the floor! Maybe some sort of message was being passed. Surely there had to be a reason! Perhaps Jimmy was telling Louie that he was his best bird-friend; who knows?

The "beak clicking" didn't happen very often—maybe once every five or six days or so—and it seemed that Louie was always the one who would start it off by squatting on the basement floor. Then Jimmy would immediately go to him and do his beak-clicking! Jake timed them with his watch and found that the longest session lasted around twenty seconds, with a few breaks of a couple seconds each.

Another concern that Jake had for little Jimmy was the flapping of Louie's enormous wings. The flapping motion caused quite a breeze! When Louie flapped his wings in front of Jimmy, then it was Jimmy's turn to squat down to avoid being blown away!

* ~ * ~ *

CHAPTER THIRTEEN

Louie Takes Off

The time was getting close for Louie's first flight; so close that Jake had to struggle with taking Louie's big cage out to the back yard every day as soon as he got home from school. He would open the cage door and Louie would hop out right away. Jake would eagerly watch, standing back and enjoying the sight of the big bird strutting about on the grass. "Flap, flap, flap, flap, flap"—then Louie would fold his wings for a few seconds and repeat the process. The five, six or more flaps he did almost lifted him to the point of take-off. Then Louie would strut around in large circles as though he owned the place, but continuously alert, watching all around in case of any danger.

Jake became rather anxious as each day came and went, increasingly sure that "tomorrow" would be the day that Louie would fly away. The time stretched to two weeks after he had made that estimation; but Louie was still around.

'He should have taken off by this time,' Jake thought. The big bird was taking so long that Jake began to think he didn't want to go; maybe he liked the free meals too much!

~ * ~

One Saturday morning, a little before lunch, Jake again had Louie's cage out in the back yard. Quite certain that Louie was strong enough; he felt that surely today would be the day. As Jake opened the cage door, Louie hopped out. As usual Jake took a little step back out of Louie's way.

When Louie started flapping his wings, Jake was surprised to see that Louie kept on flapping, but didn't go anywhere. His wings were arched in such a peculiar way that they didn't have any "lift" at all. They were "off-time" too, not flapping in unison, so that he could keep flapping and still remain on the ground.

'What is he doing?' Jake wondered. 'Surely he wants to go.' But apparently he didn't. Louie continued for longer than he had ever flapped his wings before, and then began his usual walking around in circles, his black, shiny feathers glistening in the sun. A few minutes later he repeated his exercises again and again. 'He's doing a good job of strengthening his wing muscles.' Jake thought, 'I think it's time he tried using them to fly away!'

By this time the boy was getting a bit fed up waiting for Louie to make up his mind whether to go or to stay; so he decided to go into the house for a glass of milk.

'Well,' he thought as he headed for the back door of the house, 'if he's not here when I come back out, then that will be just too bad; although I would like to say "goodbye" to him when he eventually goes.' But Jake was quite sure, going by Louie's past behavior, that there was a very good chance that the big bird would still be there.

Jake got his glass of milk and then suddenly thought of going to his room to pick up Jimmy. Jake did not know why, but he had never thought it a good idea to take his little friend outside while waiting to see if Louie would take off. He had never taken both birds out to the yard at the same time. Now it occurred to him that maybe Jimmy would also want to say "goodbye" to his big buddy!

With Jimmy on his shoulder, Jake headed back out to the yard, picking up a folding lawn chair along the way so that he could sit and watch the two birds in comfort. Strangely, when he got outside again, he was pleased to see that Louie was still there, continuing to do his exercises.

In order to get the folding chair properly set up, Jake put Jimmy down onto the short grass. No sooner had he done this, when Louie squatted low. Immediately, Jimmy rushed over and the beak-clicking started, while Jake sat and watched. It must have lasted for more than a minute this time, between little breaks. Then it was Jimmy's turn to squat down while Louie took off straight up into the air. Jake figured Louie had been waiting to say "goodbye" to his little friend.

After watching Louie for a second or two, Jake bent down to let Jimmy hop onto his fingers. Standing up and placing Jimmy on his shoulder, he looked again for Louie. At first he couldn't see the big guy. Then he spotted him. Still quite close, Louie was flying around them in large circles, just above the height of Jake's head.

Shouting, "'Bye Louie, 'bye my big friend," Jake kept his eyes on Louie, turning with him as he circled and waiting for him to fly away. Soon Louie turned and soared up into the sky.

With a massive amount of pent-up emotion, Jake suddenly realized that maybe he would never see Louie again. In almost a whisper, he barely was able to say, "'Bye Louie . . . 'bye, my big friend.... Take care now, you hear?"

~~*

CHAPTER FOURTEEN

A Happy Homecoming

Tears rolled down Jake's cheeks as he watched Louie fly away, heading for a bunch of trees far in the distance. The huge lump was back in his throat again!

'What is this feeling I have for birds that makes me so attached to them?' Jake thought. 'I had the same lump in my throat when I thought I'd lost my little Jimmy last year.'

He continued to watch Louie. Soon the raven was just a black dot in the distance. But slowly the dot started to veer to the right; then it seemed like Louie might be coming back.

'Yes, he is. Maybe he's coming back to us,' Jake hoped as Louie got closer—and closer, and lower.

Circling overhead again, Louie swooped. The next thing Jake knew was that Louie had come from behind and landed on the opposite shoulder from Jimmy. They were all three facing the same way. "Jimmy's a good boy, Jimmy's a good boy," Louie said.

"Louie's a good boy," was what Jake said back to him! 'Wow,' he was also thinking. 'I have a budgie on my left shoulder and a raven on my right shoulder!' Jake stood absolutely still. He didn't know what else to do. Not that he was scared or anything like that; just that a raven is such a BIG bird and so much heavier than his little budgie. What an experience for Jake! Louie looked even bigger when Jake slightly turned his head and found the raven just a few inches from his eyes! It was the biggest thrill of Jake's life!

'Hey, this is weird!' Jake thought. 'Here I am, with tears rolling down my face because Louie went away, and now I'm so happy he came back!'

Jake felt as if a beautiful eagle had landed on his shoulder— not a plain, old raven! He wondered where the kid had gone who was so keen to get rid of "Thing" not very long ago. Jake didn't know if Louie was going to stay around or if he was intending to fly away again for good. All Jake could do was wait and hope.

'Mom and Dad have got to see this,' was the next thing on Jake's mind. So, with a bird on each shoulder, he opened the back door and called into the house for them to "come and see this."

Jake's mom was first to arrive and her eyes opened wide in amazement. She turned her head immediately and called into the house, "George, hurry here and see this before the big bird flies away." Jake's dad quickly appeared at the back door. Then they both laughed, amazed at this wonderful spectacle!

When Jake told them of the routine with Jimmy's beak and of Louie's flight, they stood there wide-eyed in disbelief.

"Jake, try to keep him there," his dad said. "I've got to get a photo of this. I hope he doesn't fly away before I get back."

Thankfully, Louie stayed put, not making any attempt to move away. After Jake's mom and dad settled down a little, his dad said, "Okay, Son, what do you think of your big raven now?"

"Oh, Dad, I don't want him to go away anymore. I want him to stay. I think he's really cool. If he wants to stay, can I keep him?"

"Sure you can, My Boy. It seems to me that the three of you are meant to be together anyway!"

Jake knew that this was something he had no control over. Louie would go—or stay. It was all up to Louie!

Jake realized now how fond he was of the raven, and wondered if that would still be true if Louie hadn't learned to "speak" a few words? Jake also knew that it did seem to make a difference how he felt toward the big bird—he also knew it shouldn't have.

~ * ~

Jake was almost scared to take Louie outside again, but knew it was something he had to do. Every time he took the two birds out to the back yard, he was afraid that this might be the last time the big guy would be around. Perhaps someday soon Louie would just take off and keep on going. Jake just couldn't understand why a wild bird would want to stay with them when it could have all the freedom it wanted.

Louie was always very good at returning after each flight. Jake just had to yell, "Louie, Louie, Louie," and the big bird would head for Jake's house. Then, as soon as he landed (and it was always on the right shoulder facing forward), Louie would say the very same thing back, "Louie, Louie, Louie." That certainly made Jake happy. If he stayed around, Jake would find other things to teach Louie to say.

~ * ~

Jake didn't want to put Louie back into a cage after his first flight, as it seemed like he was sending the big bird to jail or someplace like that. He figured that Louie should be able to fly around the basement as much as he liked, especially seeing that Louie had chosen to remain with Jake and Jimmy.

At first, Jake's mom and dad were not too keen on this idea, but when he promised to clean up after the big bird (Louie wasn't what you would call "house-trained"), they said it would be all right! It was good, too, that the basement was large, wide open and not developed in any way.

Jake thought it was good, too, that he had the "great idea" of taking Jimmy out to the back yard at the same time that he had Louie outside. Maybe Jimmy would be just the thing to keep the big guy from flying away!

CHAPTER FIFTEEN

A Cat Wants Jimmy

Louie had become a treat to have around and Jake found out that he was also a bit of a show-off. With his huge beak Louie would pick up a small stone from the gravel driveway and up into the air he would go. Then flying around, he would swoop toward a metal garbage bin at the bottom of the yard and let the stone drop. "Bong," it would bounce off the lid and Jake would shout "Good shot, Louie." He was quite a marksman (or maybe a "marksbird")—well, "hot-shot" anyway—for he hit the bin more often than not.

On the few times that he missed, however, Louie did get a bit upset. Then, instead of doing his usual "dive bombing," he would come in rather low and go straight for the bin to make sure that he didn't miss twice in a row! He was never in a hurry to call it quits. Perhaps he considered this stone-dropping as "Louie's fun time."

After spending some time dropping stones, Louie liked to land beside Jimmy and hop around him as if he was saying, "Come on, let's go." Then up he would go again for more target practice. Whenever Louie landed, Jimmy hopped around him doing lots of "chirp, chirp, chirping" and Louie would answer with his "crawk, crawk, crawks." Jake could tell the two of them were having a really good time.

~ * ~

Although Jake enjoyed watching the two birds, he tended to get a bit bored after a while; and that's why he got careless. One Sunday afternoon he really wasn't paying attention to what was happening, and, of course, that's when things are most likely to go wrong.

The three of them were enjoying themselves in the back yard. Jimmy was hopping around, keeping Louie's attention for a while; then, all of a sudden, Louie would take off and sort of "buzz-bomb" Jimmy so that sometimes there was only a small gap between them when Louie flew in low.

Louie would never have hit Jimmy in his dives. He was always just low enough to make the little guy "freeze" in place. This was because, on Louie's way in, he would make such a noise that Jimmy, for certain, knew he was coming. He would holler

"Louie, Louie." all the time he was swooping down. That gave the little guy the message that Louie was on his way.

This is what they were doing when Jake sort-of fell behind in his "bird-sitting" duties.

Jake had to go upstairs to the bathroom, and thought that the two birds would be all right while he was gone for a minute or so. Just before he came back downstairs he glanced out of the bathroom window to have a quick look at how the two birds were doing and saw something that horrified him!

A big orange-colored cat was crouching low in the grass, almost ready to pounce on Jimmy! Jake's heart seemed to stop for a horrible instant and then, tearing down the stairs as fast as he could, he rushed into the yard. Well, what he saw then would have made him laugh if he hadn't been so scared for Jimmy.

Loudly squawking his "Louie, Louie, Louie" each time he came in for attack, Louie was holding off danger by diving almost on top of the cat. This sure helped to scare that old cat! Louie's assaults were almost continuous. He would barely take time to turn before he attacked from the opposite direction. The cat didn't know what to do.

Then Louie changed his strategy. Quickly dropping to the ground and picking up one stone after another from the gravel driveway, he proceeded to dive-bomb the cat repeatedly. This completely took the cat's attention away from Jimmy and made it focus on Louie to see what was coming next. Jake just watched, his mouth wide open in amazement.

Man, was Louie ever fast! And another thing, none of these were his usual "fun" runs. No, they were the serious "don't-miss-this-time" kind. He made sure to hit the cat with the stone every time!

Jake lost count of how many times Louie nailed the cat; it was great seeing him protect his little buddy like that!

Fortunately, the stones weren't big enough to really hurt the cat; but Jake could almost see the look on the cat's face as it continued to watch the raven, saying to itself, "No lunch is worth this much." It wasn't long before the cat took off with an angry "mrryeeouw."

Jake didn't have to do a thing to protect Jimmy. Louie had seen to it! He'd saved his little friend, Jimmy.

* ~ * ~ *

CHAPTER SIXTEEN

Jimmy Gets to Fly!

The excitement was over, or so Jake thought. He was hoping that life would settle down so he could relax a bit; but it wasn't to be.

Jake had taken the two birds out into the back yard a little later that same day since he had to pick up the stones that Louie had used earlier to scare off the cat. He knew that one of the stones could easily get picked up by the lawn mower blade and be hurled like a bullet at a person or a window. While Jake did this chore, he thought it might be good for Louie to get some more exercise.

After he finished clearing the stones, Jake sat on a chair to watch the two birds play before taking them inside. Again, he was probably relaxing a bit too much—maybe paying less than the usual attention to them—when suddenly Louie squatted down on the grass. Jimmy went very quickly to him and again the beak-tapping started. This time it was much different, though. The two birds took turns; and this time it lasted for much more than a minute. The next thing Jake knew was that Jimmy had hopped up onto Louie's back. Then suddenly UP, UP, UP into the air Louie went, taking little Jimmy with him!

"Oh no—NO—JIMMY, LOUIE ...," Jake shouted as he started to jump out of his chair. But it was useless; the birds were too far away for Jake to do anything about it anyway. He watched helplessly as Louie took Jimmy right up into the sky. "He'll fall off; he's a goner," Jake said out loud. His heart felt like it was in his throat as he watched Louie rise higher and higher into the sky with Jimmy riding "piggyback." Jake didn't want to look, but just had to. After all, his little wingless budgie was soaring sixty feet up in the air on the back of a raven!

Jake had seen Louie fly around many times before, often performing very steep turns. 'Boy,' he realized, 'if Louie does one of those turns now, little Jimmy is sure to fall off and be badly hurt or maybe even killed!'

Around they went, higher and higher, until Jake could hardly see them. Then Louie dropped, fast as an arrow out of the sky into a dive. Jake felt his heart thumping so hard it seemed to fill his whole chest.

'Why, oh, why did I want that Louie raven to stay? Now it's going to cost me my little Jimmy!' was all that Jake could think. One minute Louie was saving Jimmy from being almost eaten by a cat, and now he was putting his little life in jeopardy by his acrobatics. Jake could do nothing else but keep watching and hoping that Jimmy would be alright.

Louie swooped very close to the ground; then he went almost straight up and sharply banked by sloping sideways with his inside wing low and his outside wing high to prevent Jimmy from slipping off. Jake didn't realize this was what Louie was doing, though; so he was sure Jimmy was going to fall off. And he didn't know how to stop it.

Then suddenly it dawned on him. "Dear God, please save my little Jimmy. I don't want him to fall off and be killed." And immediately it popped into Jake's mind how to solve the problem.

"Louie, Louie, Louie." Jake shouted . . . and Louie responded right away!

*~ * ~ *

CHAPTER SEVENTEEN

Jake and His BFFs

The flying maneuvers stopped just as fast as they had started, for Louie came in, made a quick swoop around Jake's back and then both he and Jimmy landed on Jake's right shoulder!

"Louie, Louie, Louie," the big bird chirped. And, for once, Jimmy didn't have anything to say!

Jake stood there, not moving in any way—absolutely amazed! Finally, he had to sit down, for his heart was pounding so fast that it felt as if it would jump right out of his chest! It took him quite a while before he could accept the fact that his little Jimmy was all right and that his big Louie had brought Jimmy safely back home.

Well, what Jake had felt when Louie had first landed on his shoulder was great; but this was utterly awesome! Like, WOW, man! He had a bird on top of a bird on his shoulder. Unbelievable!

Jake thought about what had just happened and, when he suddenly realized what it was all about, he burst out laughing. Oh, he was so happy right then—for himself and for both birds, too!

You see, Jimmy had no wings, so Jimmy couldn't fly. Right? Jimmy would never have known what it was like to be away, high in the air, swooping and gliding; that is, unless he happened to have a flying friend like big Louie! Now Jimmy had experienced flying at last.

Jake put his fingers up to Jimmy who hopped onto them right away. Then he placed the little budgie in his usual place on his left shoulder. Looking at Louie's back, Jake could clearly see the grab marks that Jimmy had made in Louie's feathers. That told him what Jake had already suspected. Jimmy had been able to get a really good grip on Louie's back. Otherwise he, most likely, would have fallen off at the very start of the flight!

Yes, Louie was smart all right. What other bird would know how to take a wingless budgie up for a spin? And Jake realized that it was good Louie was as big and tough as he was, for he didn't seem to mind what must have been some painful scratches on his skin under those feathers.

It also seemed that Louie hadn't really gone very far beyond the edge of the yard during this thrill-filled flight. Jake wondered if Jimmy would want to go back up again for another spin sometime. He also wondered if he would *let* him. If Jimmy was willing to take a chance on Louie, should Jake be willing to do the same? He would have to do some thinking about that and maybe talk it over with his parents. He loved his little Jimmy too much to consider risking his little life for the sake of a thrill!

~ * ~

'Well,' Jake thought, 'the library book did say that ravens were smart, didn't it?' And, boy, was he ever pleased now that he had such a large, smart bird!

Jake was so happy. The times he had spent earlier wishing that Louie would fly away and take his "supposed" problems with him were now a thing of the past. Jake finally realized that he loved his Big Louie every bit as much as he loved his Little Jimmy! In fact, the three of them loved each other. What could be better?

Jake looked forward to many more good times ahead with his two BFFs—not only his *Best Friends Forever*, but also his *Best Feathered Friends*!

THE END

ABOUT THE CO-AUTHORS

Ian Moore-Morrans, the main author of this book, is presently 82 years old. He lives with his wife, editor and co-author, Gayle Moore-Morrans, and their dog, a shih-poo named Misty, in Vernon, British Columbia. He is a retired machinist who emigrated from Scotland to Canada in 1965 with his late wife Mary and two young daughters, Audrey and Shirley. Ian had always wanted to be an author, but life, music-making and work had come in the way of fulfilling that dream. Finally, at age 63, he started writing what was to become this very book. He went on to write many more stories.

Gayle Moore-Morrans is a retired magazine and program editor who started writing at age 8 when she wrote and illustrated her first "book" about a new puppy whose surprise birth to their dog, Lady, had delighted her and her two younger sisters when they were growing up in North Dakota. (She still has the original and only copy of that handmade "book.") She has continued to write throughout life, both in her work capacity and in documenting personal and family happenings. Best of all, though, she likes to edit. She began to edit Ian's writings about a year after she and Ian were married in September 2003.

Gayle and her late husband, Gus, both Americans, had lived in Germany for 18 years where they adopted their two children, Gwynne and Garen. In 1983 they returned to the States and then, nine months later, immigrated to Winnipeg, Manitoba. Gus went onto disability retirement in 1992 as Gayle began working for Evangelical Lutheran Women of the Evangelical Lutheran Church in Canada.

Gayle was widowed in 1996 and, six years later, met newly-widowed Ian. At their initial meeting, besides being attracted to each other, they were intrigued that Ian was an author and Gayle was an editor. They began to envision living and working together and were married in September 2003.

HOW THIS BOOK CAME TO BE

Gayle presently maintains a blog entitled "**Ian Moore-Morrans, Scottish-Canadian Author & Gayle Moore-Morrans, American-Canadian Editor, Author & Blogger**" at **ianmooremorrans.com**. Readers are invited to visit that blog, click on the "Follow" button and continue to receive email messages announcing new blogposts.

Following are excerpts from that blog in which Gayle and Ian initially previewed draft chapters of this book, suggested graphics and quoted excerpts from their next-to-be published book which help to tell the story of how *Jake, Little Jimmy & Big Louie* came to be.

Ian describes this book's beginnings in the following excerpt from *Came To Canada, Eh? Continuing a Scottish Immigrant's Story*, which is next in Gayle's queue of "to-be-edited-and-published works," written by Ian Moore-Morrans with Gayle Moore-Morrans, © copyright 2013. To set the scene, Ian and his late wife have just moved back to Winnipeg (for the 4th or 5th time). Ian is 63 years old and decides to finally do what he has always wanted to do but never before found time for.

My whole life I had always wanted to write stories, but the situation was never the way I wanted it to be. Whenever, for example, I wrote a letter to anyone in the Old Country, I would end up sending about 14-16 pages—and I would get one page in reply. Finally, at age 63, I said to myself, 'Ian, if you don't start to write now, then you'll never do it.' So I sat down and, over a period of three evenings, wrote "My Friend Jimmy." It was a children's story about a budgie that had no wings—just 16 pages. But I had to write everything longhand. I asked Audrey to keep her eyes open for a used electric typewriter for me.

"What do you want an electric typewriter for, Dad? You'll be wasting your time. Why don't you get a used computer? That'll do the same thing for you, only better."

Oh, that was a terrible word to use in front of an old codger like me—a computer? Sudden terror at the thought of even having one in front of me! Well, she eventually managed to convince me that that is what I should get.

It helped that Audrey offered, "Do you want me to look for one for you? You can pick one up dirt cheap, Dad."

It was a 286, black and white monitor, no hard drive, just two 3.5" floppy disks; but it was a start. I then became a little more ambitious—going to the library and getting out one of those foldout learn-to-type books that stands upright on edge (like a pyramid) and I started to learn to touch type. Me, an old . . . well, something. And I was improving too— starting to type simple sentences without looking at the keyboard. Pretty soon I got myself a 386 computer, then later it was up to a 486, and then a Pentium! Hey, who was that guy who said that the 286 was all he would ever need? I got the Mavis Beacon typing course (on a CD) and was able to calculate that I was up to more than 20 words a minute, even allowing for errors! 'Not bad for an oldie,' I thought.

While I was improving on my typing, I rewrote my children's story, and kept editing it until it started to look a lot better. I changed some of the contents and then sent it away to a publisher, knowing full well that he would grab it and tell me that it was the very best children's story he had ever read. ... Some hope! Soon I could just about paper the wall with rejections.

'Never mind,' I thought, 'where there's life, there's hope.' I put the story on file and went on to write other stories, thinking that I'd give "My Friend Jimmy" a try again at a later date. (Little was I to know that the later date would be lots later—almost 20 years!)

"AM I A CO-AUTHOR OR JUST THE EDITOR?"

To explain how she came to be a co-author of this book, here is an excerpt from a blog post Gayle wrote in reply to another author/blogger who had collaborated on her late mother's writings:

I've put aside the pile of writing I've done over the years, mostly on spiritual insights and family history and feel it is my "labor of love" to try to get the rest of Ian's writings edited and published. However, as you've found with your mother's writings I have been grappling with the fact that I no longer can ask Ian to do re-writes when I feel they are warranted. Like you said with your mother's work, "I began to make changes and what I was doing was much more than editing." Ian and I have discussed how to address the authorship of the next book which I hope will be coming out soon. Granted, he is the main author. He originally wrote the children's story, nursed it through a number of revisions over the years and had sent it to several publishers even before I met him. It was hung up on the need for editing though. I now have done the editing but have also made a number of changes in the story and added a spiritual component to it which Ian had hinted at but which I felt needed expanding. It no longer is just the story that Ian wrote. I've also recruited our 8-year-old great-granddaughter to do the illustrations for the book and have extensively adjusted those illustrations using Microsoft Paint to make them more consistent and the characters more uniform. So how do we identify the authorship of the book? Ian and I have discussed this and have tossed around listing a co-authorship or a "with" authorship such as "by Ian Moore-Morrans with Gayle Moore-Morrans." We've thought that perhaps the former gives too much credit to me and perhaps the latter makes it look as if Ian had a ghost writer (which certainly isn't the case).

IAN AND THE "REAL" JIMMY

In the following excerpts from the yet-to-be-published memoir, *Came to Canada, Eh? Continuing a Scottish Immigrant's Story*, Ian describes receiving his real-life bird, a cockatiel he named "Jimmy." This should give readers an insight into some of the things Ian learned about raising a bird and teaching it to speak and whistle. He later added some of these ideas to *Jake, Little Jimmy & Big Louie*. Having read the book, perhaps readers will notice that certain things Ian experienced with his cockatiel, Jimmy, later were used in the characterizations of Little Jimmy and also of Big Louie.

This 1998 photo shows Ian and Jimmy, his cockatiel.

From *Came to Canada, Eh?*, written about Ian's time in Creighton, Saskatchewan, 1997-1998:

Mary and I went down to Winnipeg to spend Christmas with Audrey and Eugene and our three grandchildren, Tammy, Calan and Ainsley in 1997. Then, since Mary and I had been married on the 29th of December, we returned home to Creighton to celebrate our anniversary. We were at Shirley and Brien's house for a quiet evening on our wedding anniversary when Shirley suddenly appeared carrying a great big bird cage.

Inside was a beautiful, young cockatiel. He and the lovely cage were being presented to us from our two daughters, their husbands and all five grandchildren, including young Ian and Tiffany. I was invited to take the bird out of its cage and hold him on my hand. He came with no bother and Shirley asked me what I was going to call him (it). Without any hesitation I said 'Jimmy' (after the little budgie in my unpublished children's book, not caring what sex the bird was!). He was such a lovely surprise gift for both of us. And we found out later that he really was a 'he.'

Jimmy took quite a lot of looking after, for I had to feed him egg almost continuously, and clean his cage almost continuously, too! He was on the egg diet a long time, longer than he should have been. Brien had obtained Jimmy from a friend at work who bred them. From what Brien learned, Jimmy should have been on seed when he was still enjoying his egg. I had bought some seed for him, but he didn't seem ready for it. When I was cooking for him, I would generally put two, sometimes three eggs in the pot and boil them hard, storing them in the fridge, for Jimmy seemed to be always hungry. I would cut off a little bit and wrap the remainder for later, making sure that Jimmy also got some of the yolk (that is what he went for first) along with some white. In the beginning I'd chop the egg up for him, but I soon found that doing so was a complete waste of time, for his little sharp beak would slice through the soft egg just like butter.

Soon I set about teaching the bird things to say and whistle. Being a musician, I don't think it is bragging to say that I'm a pretty good whistler as I'm able to do quite a bit of fancy stuff like grace notes, triplets, warbles and different things— a lot of stuff that I did on the trumpet. Soon our bird was saying 'Jimmy's a good boy' (just like in my little story), 'Hi Ian, wot's up?,' 'Hello, Mary,' 'I love Shirley' and so forth. He also started whistling the verse of "Bonnie Jean" from Brigadoon that I was rehearsing for my solo at our upcoming concert in Flin Flon. (I didn't teach him this, he just picked it up while I was whistling it around the house and going through the words in my head.) In addition, I taught him to whistle the first part of 'The Mexican Hat Dance'; the bugle call that goes, 'You gotta get up; you gotta get up; you gotta get up in the morning,' a series of notes from a 'custom' car horn, and a silly something we used to sing in Scotland when I was a wee boy that ended with 'Wee Bobby Geachy's --- white drawers.' The latter bit used the popular rhythm that everyone knows: 'DAH dah dah DAH dah – DAH! DAH!' However, what I taught Jimmy varied in that I substituted a wolf whistle for the last two notes (the last 'DAH! DAH!'). Jimmy really did it superbly. (Sometimes I would whistle the first bit and he would answer with the wolf whistle and other times it would be reversed, with Jimmy starting.)

Jimmy really performed to perfection the day I was dressed in my kilt outfit just prior to leaving the house for the dress rehearsal of the show I was in. Jimmy's cage was in the dining room and as I passed the door opening that would allow him to see me, he went, "Wheeet-wheeoo"—a perfect, long, wolf whistle. I burst out laughing. It was like he did it intentionally, his timing was so right. My answer was, "Hey, Funny Guy. You've never seen a Scotsman in a kilt before?'

Ian and Jimmy "schmoozing."

From *Came to Canada, Eh?*, written about Ian's time in Flin Flon, Manitoba 1998-2000:

I've never trimmed Jimmy's wings, as later I got to thinking that by doing so I was making him just like the little budgie in my story "My Friend Jimmy" who was born without any wings. (Trimming of the wings is quite common practice among people who have pet birds.)

Jimmy flies all over the house, generally when he is looking for me. His cage is only closed at night when I'm going to bed or if the kitchen stove is on. That's because one day he landed on the hot griddle as I was making some French toast for lunch. Luckily he landed on the soggy-eggy-bread. And, no, I didn't eat that slice; I gave it to Mary. (Readers are supposed to laugh here!)

If I'm in the kitchen making tea or a no-stove-on lunch, he comes looking for me and lands on my shoulder. If he is strolling on the living room floor and I make sort-of kissy noises with my lips, he will fly up onto my shoulder, just like he was a little dog. Which reminds me, he also loves to play with our dog, Peppy. And Peppy loves to play with him, too.

If I whistle one of our musical pieces, especially "Bonnie Jean" he will immediately fly up to my shoulder. He does so many interesting things; I call him my little treasure. I should also mention that he isn't toilet trained in any way, so I have to watch where he "keechs." (That's Gaelic for s--- but doesn't sound quite as crude.) His doo-doos are generally little round things that are easily picked up with a leaf of toilet paper. If he "goes" while he is walking on the counter top, then I have to sanitize it with a bleach solution right away. I did try putting a diaper on him but he looked ridiculous and couldn't fly very well! (I do hope that sometimes readers don't take me too seriously.)

If I am going down to the basement the odd afternoon to have a quiet nap in my old reclining chair, he will come with me and sit on my chest, about two inches from my chin. Then we will both go to sleep. Whenever I am sitting at the computer, he may be on the floor and I will feel him climbing my jogging suit pant leg. Then he may sit on my right knee, tuck his little head into his wing and go to sleep. (When he does that, I won't disturb him, even if I want to use the bathroom! I just sit, work, and wait until he wakes). I have added quite a lot of wood to the inside of his cage, making it more comfortable for him. For example, I put in a couple of small proper tree branches about an inch thick, and added more substantial perches for him, plus an indoor swimming pool. Different little things that make his life a little more pleasant.

I can give him a toothpick and he grabs it with his beak, then he gets hold of it with his left claw, and you would swear blind that he was cleaning his teeth. He never gets covered at night the way many other birds do. He stays quiet until I get up (generally around nine o'clock). Then I go to his cage, prop open his cage door and say, "Good morning, Jimmy." He is generally heading for that door as I'm getting ready to open it. Then the first thing I usually hear from him is "Bonnie Jean"! (I can almost bet on it, as soon as he is out of his cage). Yep, he is definitely my little treasure and I'm very glad he happened into my life.

You would have to spend a full day in my home to get to know the real Jimmy; he is so full of surprises. And the things we do together you would not believe. There's no way I would ever get another cockatiel after Jimmy goes (if he goes before I do), for I'm sure that there's not another bird in this world that could be so much in tune with me and me with him. (He has to come to my lips to have breakfast with me. He knows I'm eating, gets to me wherever he is and won't give me any peace until I let him have some!)

I had my computer in the basement during the summer as it was nice and cool down there. As I typed, he stayed with me, climbing all over. Because the basement was rather dark I needed the lights on. There was one bright bulb in the wrong place, which I intended to move (eventually). To combat this necessary bright light, I wore a cap with a sunshade. Jimmy was on my shoulder and then climbed up to the top of my head. As I was typing away, not bothering too much as to what he was doing, suddenly I saw his little head, upside down, three inches in front of my eyes, looking at me over the edge of my cap! Well, I just broke up, he looked so funny!

© 2013 ian moore-morrans

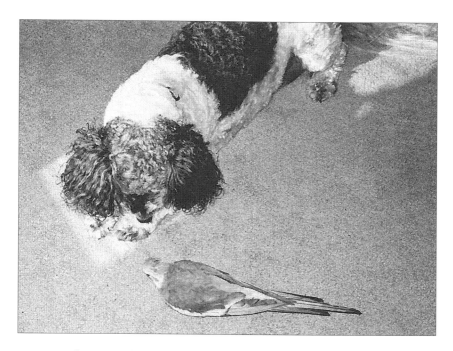

Peppy, the poodle, and Jimmy, the cockatiel, became great friends and loved to play together.

From *Came to Canada, Eh?,* written about Ian's time in New Glasgow, Nova Scotia, 2001:

My cockatoo Jimmy became a problem for us. I found out that cockatoos usually live for about 28-30 years. I figured I probably would not outlive him and didn't want him to have to suffer my loss in his old age. Jimmy and I had become very friendly with a family living close to us. Every time the kids came to our house they spent more time with Jimmy than they did with me and, of course, he just loved the attention.

Their dad was always at me to sell Jimmy to him as the whole family thought he was the very best pet they had ever encountered.

I needed some work done on the roof to fix some tiles that would soon be causing me a problem and this chap was very capable. So I offered to give them Jimmy if he would repair my roof. He readily agreed.

As I said "goodbye" to my little friend, I figured he wouldn't miss me much. However, I sure missed him for a long time! My little dog Peppy became even more precious to me after the loss of my Jimmy.

© *2013 ian moore-morrans*

ABOUT OUR WEE YINS' PART IN THIS BOOK

(Note: the Scots-English word for children, youngsters or literally "wee ones" is "wee yins.")

Included herewith are excerpts from some of Gayle's blogposts on www.ianmooremorrans.com.

December 21, 2012: *As a Christmas gift for our great-grandchildren, especially for the oldest two, Leland (11) and Hannah (7), we are going to begin blogging a children's chapter book for ages 7-12, that Ian began to write some years ago but has not yet published. We're hoping that Leland and Hannah will enjoy reading it, will give us some feedback on the story and perhaps even read it to their younger siblings and cousins. [We have seven great-grandchildren in Manitoba as well as a young grandson in Norway. The other grandchildren are in their late 20s and 30s, as are Gayle's children. Ian's children are in their 50s.] We're hoping they will also like the book, even though it was originally written for children. Grandma Gayle liked it and she is 70!*

Readers of this blog are also invited to share the story with their children, grandchildren and great-grandchildren, if they are lucky enough to have some. We're hoping that

Hannah, who is a wonderful little artist, may even want to draw some pictures that may eventually go into the published book.

March 12, 2013: ***Wow! A Recommendation from Our "Age-Appropriate Consultant"***

We're still glowing from our great-grandson's very positive endorsement of the book so far. Here is the message we received from our 12-year-old great-grandson Leland. Thank you, Leland. We don't think we've ever had such a great review!"

"Hey grandma and grandpa i just finished reading the first six chapters of that book you sent me and it was one of the best books I've ever read!!! and im also starting to draw the picture for the second chapter, but i just started it because i was reading for about an hour so my eyes are really stressed out right now so im going to go to bed and i will continue tomorrow!

"but it is a really good book so-far.

"Love, Leland"

January 13, 2014:
I, Gayle, am at present
enhancing/editing some
illustrations for our new
children's book ("Jake,
Little Jimmy & Big
Louie"). Our illustrator
is our eight-year-old
great-granddaughter. Here's a drawing that Hannah made
of herself and Grandma Gayle the last time we were
together.

We don't have the luxury of living in the same place but
Hannah's grandmother (daughter Audrey) has read
through the draft chapters with her and then oversees her
drawings for each chapter, scans them in and sends us the
JPGs. Hannah has done some darling illustrations for the
book but we find that her depictions of the leading
characters are not always consistent from illustration to
illustration. I am now using Microsoft Word Paint to adjust
them for a uniformity of sorts, allowing me to make the boy
and the birds more consistent without losing her child's
perspective. I will then rescan the edited pictures at a
resolution high enough for printing in the book. It's fun but
painstaking.

August 19, 2014: ***Celebrating Family.*** *We have decided to dedicate our next book, a children's book, Jake, Little Jimmy & Big Louie, to the **eleven children in our lives**, three of them born since we first started blogging the book. They are our youngsters (or "wee yins," as Ian would call them in his Scottish vernacular).*

In the center is a picture of Ian signing a stack of his books and one of Gayle busy at one of her Location Writing sessions. We are surrounded by photos of these very special children who make up our blended family: from top left and clockwise, Leland, Hannah, Logan, Eva, Gustav, Haylee, Brayden, Alex, Lexi, Madison and Caleigh. We love them all!

37612423R00077

Made in the USA
Charleston, SC
15 January 2015